T0048254

BOOK OF BEGINNING TRUMPET SOLOS

Edited by **Fred Mills** and **Ron Romm**
of The Canadian Brass

■

All Selections Performed by
Fred Mills and **Ron Romm** on trumpet,
and pianist Bill Casey

■

Plus Piano Accompaniments Only
Arranged by Bill Boyd

CONTENTS

* Ron Romm, trumpet, on recording.
** Fred Mills, trumpet, on recording.

The instrument pictured on the cover is a CB10 Trumpet from The Canadian Brass Collection,
a line of professional brass instruments marketed by The Canadian Brass.

Photo: Gordon Janowiak

To access audio visit:
www.halleonard.com/mylibrary

Enter Code
3771-1497-3721-5560

7777 W. BLUEMOUND RD. P.O. BOX 13819 MILWAUKEE, WI 53213

www.canadianbrass.com
www.halleonard.com

Dear Fellow Brass Player:

We might be just a little biased, but we believe that playing a brass instrument is one of the most positive activities that anyone can pursue. Whether you're 8 years old or 60 years old, the ability to play a horn automatically creates opportunities of playing with other people in bands, orchestras and ensembles throughout your life. But to keep yourself in shape and to better your playing, it's important to regularly work at solos. You might perform a contest solo for school, or play for a church service, or just for your family in the living room. Here's a book full of solos, in varied styles, that we think you'll enjoy learning.

All this music has been recorded for you on the companion cassette. On side A each of us in The Canadian Brass has recorded all the pieces in this collection on our respective instruments, letting you hear how the music sounds. On side B you will find piano accompaniments for you to use in your practice, or if you wish, to perform with. The recordings of the solos that we have made should be used only as a guide in studying a piece. We certainly didn't go into these recording sessions with the idea of trying to create any kind of "definitive performances" of this music. There is no such thing as a definitive performance anyway. Each musician, being a unique individual, will naturally always come up with a slightly different rendition of a piece of music. We often find that students are timid about revealing their own ideas and personalities when going beyond the notes on the page in making music. After you've practiced for weeks on a piece of music, and have mastered all the technical requirements, you certainly have earned the right to play it in the way you think it sounds best! It may not be the way your friend would play it, or the way The Canadian Brass would play it. But you will have made the music your own, and that's what counts.

Good luck and Happy Brass Playing!
The Canadian Brass

FRED MILLS had an extensive performing career that preceded his joining The Canadian Brass. He grew up in Guelph, Ontario. After graduating from the Juilliard School of Music, he became principal trumpet under conductor Leopold Stokowski in both the American and Houston Symphonies. He also performed under Pablo Casals at the Casals Festival, and has played at the Marlboro Music Festival. For six years Fred was principal trumpet of the New York City Opera orchestra. Following this, he returned to Canada to take a position as principal trumpet of the then newly formed National Arts Centre Orchestra in Ottawa. In 1996, after 23 years with the ensemble, Fred chose to come off the road and lend his expertise to students at the University of Georgia.

RON ROMM was a child prodigy as a trumpet player, beginning his career as a soloist at the age of ten. By twelve, he was a member of his family's band; by age eighteen he was performing regularly with the Los Angeles Philharmonic. Ron attended the Juilliard School, and while in New York established himself as a top freelance trumpeter in the city, performing with everything from the New York Philharmonic to the Radio City Music Hall Symphony Orchestra to Broadway shows (like Sondheim's *Company*) to the circus tours and ice shows. Ron joined The Canadian Brass in 1971, just when the group had been together about a year. Although he has little time for performing outside the extensive Canadian Brass concert schedule, he is sought after as a pre-eminent soloist in many musical styles:

BILL CASEY, pianist, grew up in Atlanta, and holds degrees in piano from Louisiana State University and the University of Missouri at Kansas City. He was assistant editor on the new G. Schirmer Opera Anthology, and has recorded several other albums for Hal Leonard. He resides in Kansas City, where he runs a music school for piano and voice students, as well as continuing to perform as both a pianist and singer.

CANADIAN BRASS BLUES

Bill Boyd

YANKEE DOODLE

Traditional American

STREETS OF LAREDO

American Folksong (adapted from old Irish air)

ODE TO JOY

Adapted from Symphony No. 9
by Ludwig van Beethoven

AMERICA

Words by Samuel F. Smith
Music by Henry Carey

CARNIVAL OF VENICE

Julius Benedict

THE RIDDLE SONG

English ballad

FINLANDIA

Jean Sibelius

CANADIAN BRASS BLUES

TRUMPET

Bill Boyd

YANKEE DOODLE

Traditional American

STREETS OF LAREDO

American Folksong (adapted from old Irish air)

Moderately

ODE TO JOY

Adapted from Symphony No. 9
by Ludwig van Beethoven

Moderately

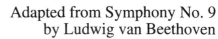

AMERICA

Words by Samuel F. Smith
Music by Henry Carey

CARNIVAL OF VENICE

Julius Benedict

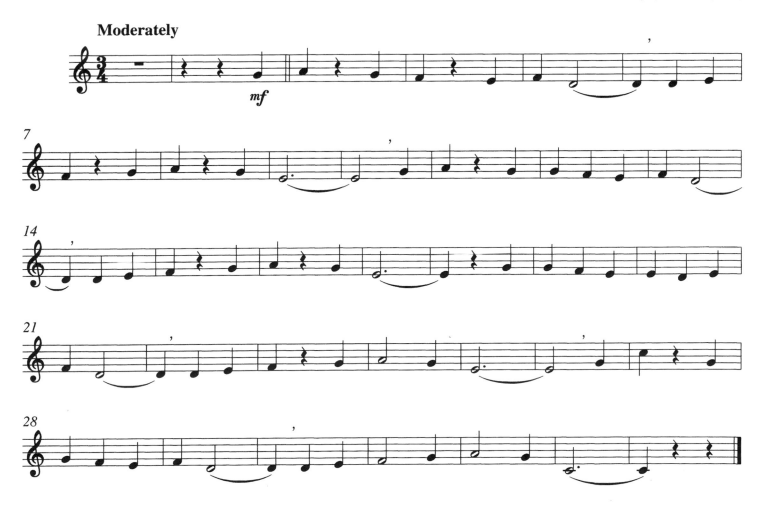

THE RIDDLE SONG

English ballad

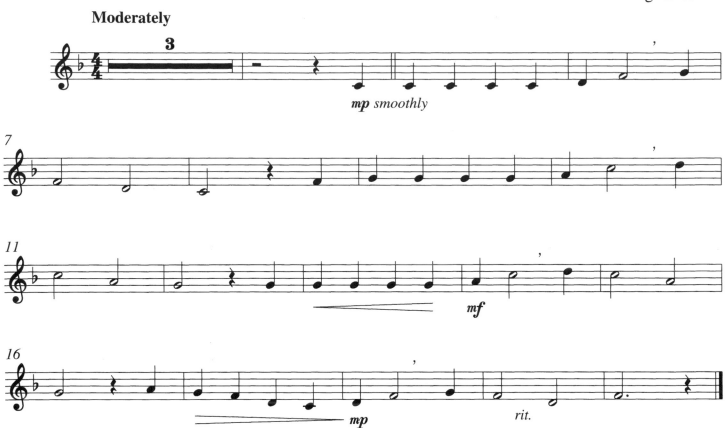

FINLANDIA

Jean Sibelius

AMAZING GRACE

Words by John Newton
Traditional American melody

THE SKATERS

Emil Wauldteufel

6

MARINE'S HYMN

Words by unknown marine (1847)
Music by Jacques Offenbach

TAKE ME OUT TO THE BALL GAME

Words by Jack Norworth
Music by Albert von Tilzer

SONG OF THE VOLGA BOATMAN

Russian Folksong

THE CRUEL WAR IS RAGING

American Folksong

DOXOLOGY

Words by Thomas Ken
Music by Louis Bourgéois

GIVE MY REGARDS TO BROADWAY

Words and Music by George M. Cohan

Moderately

JUST A CLOSER WALK

Words and Music by Red Foley

Slowly

AMAZING GRACE

Words by John Newton
Traditional American melody

THE SKATERS

Emil Wauldteufel

MARINE'S HYMN

Words by unknown marine (1847)
Music by Jacques Offenbach

TAKE ME OUT TO THE BALL GAME

Words by Jack Norworth
Music by Albert von Tilzer

SONG OF THE VOLGA BOATMAN

Russian Folksong

THE CRUEL WAR IS RAGING

American Folksong

DOXOLOGY

Words by Thomas Ken
Music by Louis Bourgéois

GIVE MY REGARDS TO BROADWAY

Words and Music by George M. Cohan

JUST A CLOSER WALK

Words and Music by Red Foley